W9-AYR-483

HARDWOOD GREATS
PRO BASKETBALL'S BEST PLAYERS

GIANNIS ANTETOKOUNMPO

HARDWOOD GREATS

PRO BASKETBALL'S BEST PLAYERS

CHRIS PAUL

GIANNIS ANTETOKOUNMPO

JAMES HARDEN

KEVIN DURANT

LEBRON JAMES

PAUL GEORGE

RUSSELL WESTBROOK

STEPHEN CURRY

HARDWOOD GREATS
PRO BASKETBALL'S BEST PLAYERS

GIANNIS ANTETOKOUNMPO

DONALD PARKER

MASON CREST
PHILADELPHIA
MIAMI

Mason Crest
450 Parkway Drive, Suite D
Broomall, Pennsylvania 19008
(866) MCP-BOOK (toll-free)
www.masoncrest.com

Copyright © 2020 by Mason Crest, an imprint of National Highlights, Inc. All rights reserved. No part of this publication may be reproduced or transmitted in any form or by any means, electronic or mechanical, including photocopying, recording, taping, or any information storage and retrieval system, without permission from the publisher.

First printing
9 8 7 6 5 4 3 2 1

ISBN (hardback) 978-1-4222-4411-1
ISBN (series) 978-1-4222- 4344-2
ISBN (ebook) 978-1-4222- 7401-9

Cataloging-in-Publication Data on file with the Library of Congress

Developed and Produced by National Highlights Inc.
Editor: Andrew Luke
Interior and cover design: Annalisa Gumbrecht, Studio Gumbrecht
Production: Michelle Luke

QR CODES AND LINKS TO THIRD-PARTY CONTENT

You may gain access to certain third-party content ("Third-Party Sites") by scanning and using the QR Codes that appear in this publication (the "QR Codes"). We do not operate or control in any respect any information, products, or services on such Third-Party Sites linked to by us via the QR Codes included in this publication, and we assume no responsibility for any materials you may access using the QR Codes. Your use of the QR Codes may be subject to terms, limitations, or restrictions set forth in the applicable terms of use or otherwise established by the owners of the Third-Party Sites. Our linking to such Third-Party Sites via the QR Codes does not imply an endorsement or sponsorship of such Third-Party Sites or the information, products, or services offered on or through the Third-Party Sites, nor does it imply an endorsement or sponsorship of this publication by the owners of such Third-Party Sites.

CONTENTS

KEY ICONS TO LOOK FOR:

 Words to Understand: These words with their easy-to-understand definitions will increase the reader's understanding of the text while building vocabulary skills.

 Sidebars: This boxed material within the main text allows readers to build knowledge, gain insights, explore possibilities, and broaden their perspectives by weaving together additional information to provide realistic and holistic perspectives.

 Educational Videos: Readers can view videos by scanning our QR codes, providing them with additional educational content to supplement the text. Examples include news coverage, moments in history, speeches, iconic sports moments, and much more!

 Text-Dependent Questions: These questions send the reader back to the text for more careful attention to the evidence presented there.

 Research Projects: Readers are pointed toward areas of further inquiry connected to each chapter. Suggestions are provided for projects that encourage deeper research and analysis.

Series Glossary of Key Terms: This back-of-the-book glossary contains terminology used throughout this series. Words found here increase the reader's ability to read and comprehend higher-level books and articles in this field.

WORDS TO UNDERSTAND

ascension: Rising from a lower level or degree

gesture: Something said or done by way of formality or courtesy, as a symbol or token, or for its effect on the attitudes of others

integral: Essential to completeness

venerable: Calling forth respect through age, character, and attainments

CHAPTER 1

GREATEST MOMENTS

GIANNIS ANTETOKOUNMPO'S NBA CAREER

Giannis Antetokounmpo has come a long way to become one of the best players in the National Basketball Association (NBA). His parents worked hard to provide a better life for their family and opportunities to achieve their personal dreams and goals. At six feet eleven inches (2.11 m) and 241 pounds (109 kg), most things are within Antetokounmpo's considerable reach, including the dream life he is currently living. Since being drafted by the Milwaukee Bucks in 2013 with the 15th overall pick, Antetokounmpo has helped breathe new life into this **venerable** franchise, leading it to three postseason appearances in his six-year career.

Antetokounmpo has become not only an **integral** part of the Bucks's winning formula, but he has also gained recognition as a fearsome competitor

Antetokounmpo has quickly turned himself into a genuine MVP threat.

who has grown into both his body and the professional game. This was evident with the 2019 NBA All-Star game, for which Antetokounmpo received the highest number of votes in the Eastern Conference and was named team captain. He is only 24 years old and has a desire to not only play his entire career in Milwaukee but to also bring back a championship, something that has eluded the franchise since 1971.

Antetokounmpo has been honored as an All-Star game starter three times and named to the All-NBA team twice in his career. He is also a recipient of the league's Most Improved Player award (2017), when he was also named to the All-Defensive team. Antetokounmpo has continued to improve his game at every level, averaging nearly 1,489 points, 658 rebounds, and 330 assists a season. With more than 8,000 points scored in his career he is on the doorstep of reaching the 10,000 points scored club, something he should be able to accomplish in the 2019–2020 season.

Antetokounmpo did not take the same path to the NBA followed by other players in the league. He grew up in Greece (his nickname is "The Greek Freak") and was not exposed to a system of organized basketball at the high school, college, or professional levels. Antetokounmpo was exposed to organized play by chance while playing in pick-up games with his brothers on the playgrounds of Athens. This lack of access did not stop him from qualifying for a local semiprofessional and professional club in Athens, and the exposure got Antetokounmpo noticed by NBA scouts, ultimately resulting in his being drafted in the first round.

Antetokounmpo's full potential is yet unknown as he continues to develop into one of the game's greats. Time will tell where Antetokounmpo ranks in the history of the NBA. One thing for certain is the league has rarely seen a player of his size with the ability to play all five positions on the court.

ANTETOKOUNMPO'S GREATEST CAREER MOMENTS

HERE IS A LIST OF

SOME OF THE CAREER

FIRSTS AND GREATEST

ACHIEVEMENTS DURING

HIS TIME IN THE NBA:

Antetokounmpo
is a three-time
NBA All-Star.

Antetokounmpo takes his game to the next level as he is named a starter for the Eastern Conference in the 2017 NBA All-Star game.

NAMED TEAM CAPTAIN OF EASTERN CONFERENCE ALL-STARS

Antetokounmpo was named as a starter in his third consecutive All-Star game in 2019. This accomplishment symbolized his **ascension** to the top of the list as one of the league's best players. Antetokounmpo received the most votes in the conference, earning him the right to be named team captain along with LeBron James, who was named team captain for the West. The honor included an opportunity to draft the teammates he wanted to play alongside, which included Stephen Curry who ended up feeding him a brilliant pass for two of Antetokounmpo's game-high 38 points.

His 38-point effort may not have been enough to win the 2019 NBA All-Star game, but it was enough for Antetokounmpo to be the leading scorer in the game.

NAMED 2017 NBA MOST IMPROVED PLAYER

Antetokounmpo's first All-Star game appearance followed a huge increase in pay that he received from the Bucks after the great season he turned in to lift the team to a 42-win, 38-loss record and a sixth seed in the Eastern Conference NBA playoffs. Antetokounmpo averaged more than 22 points a game for the first time in his career in 2017 (22.9), pulled down 8.8 rebounds a game and dished out 5.4 assists a game, helping his team reach the postseason. He was also an All-Star, second-team All-NBA, and second-team All-Defensive, all of which helped further justify his being named Most Improved Player.

These highlights of "The Greek Freak" show why Antetokounmpo was named Kia NBA's Most Improved Player for the 2016–2017 season.

NAMED TO 2017 NBA ALL-DEFENSIVE SECOND TEAM

The 2016–2017 season was quite a season for Antetokounmpo. He received numerous honors and recognition and improved his game to help his team earn a good playoff seeding. This improvement was driven by his defensive efforts in support of his outstanding offensive numbers. Antetokounmpo turned in a season that included top 20 finishes in the league in blocks (fifth with 151), steals (ninth with 131), and defensive rebounds (13th with 558). This effort not only helped his Bucks win, but it also helped Antetokounmpo secure a spot on an NBA All-Defensive team for the season.

Whether it was stealing the ball, blocking shots, or grabbing defensive rebounds, Antetokounmpo excelled in the 2016–2017 season, turning in a spectacular All-Defensive performance filled with plays like this one against Kevin Durant and the Golden State Warriors, November 19, 2016.

NAMED TO ALL-NBA TEAM FOR THE FIRST TIME

The All-NBA teams recognize the best players in the NBA for the season. These players are traditionally those considered good enough to be named Most Valuable Player (MVP) for the league. The season that Antetokounmpo turned in for 2016–2017 certainly placed him in the discussion as a possible MVP candidate (Russell Westbrook of Oklahoma City won the award). Antetokounmpo's season as a forward was recognized for honor as a member of the All-NBA team in 2017, along with other second-teamers (by position): Rudy Gobert (center), Kevin Durant (forward), Stephen Curry (guard), and Isaiah Thomas (guard).

These top 10 plays from the 2016–2017 season show why Antetokounmpo was named to the All-NBA second team.

6

NBA MOST VALUABLE PLAYER

The 2016-2017 season, Antetokounmpo's fourth in the league, is when he joined the ranks of the league's best players with an All-Star caliber campaign. In the 2018-2019 season, he established himself as a dominant force in the league, posting career highs in points per game, assists and shooting percentage. Antetokounmpo also finished third in the league in scoring, sixth in rebounding and 10th in blocks to earn NBA MVP honors. He was also an NBA All-Defensive First Team selection. Upon receiving the trophy at the awards ceremony, he tearfully thanked his family, and especially his deceased father, saying, "Everyday that I step on the floor, I always think about my dad, and that motivates me and pushes me to play hard".

Antetokounmpo led Milwaukee to 60 wins and the best record in the league, only the second time the Bucks have ever been the NBA's best team.

This video by Antetokounmpo sponsor Nike nicely sums up his unlikely rise to the very top of the NBA.

Antetokounmpo accomplished something in the 2016–2017 NBA season that no player has ever done before. He finished the season ranked in the top 20 of each of the major statistical categories (assists, blocks, rebounds, steals, and total points scored). For the season, Antetokounmpo scored 1,832 points, good enough for 14th in the league. He also grabbed 700 rebounds (15th) and stole the ball from opponents 131 times, good for ninth. His 434 assists were good for 18th in the NBA that season, and 151 blocks ranked Antetokounmpo fifth. These numbers helped win him the league's Most Improved Player award

EAST 1ST RD - BUCKS LEAD 1-0

MILWAUKEE **97**   TORONTO **100**

BONUS   BONUS

TORYCLIPS © *GDFACTORYCLIPS*

Highlights of a season that saw Antetokounmpo become the first player in the history of the league to finish in the top 20 on points, rebounds, assists, blocks, and steals.

FIRST CAREER TRIPLE-DOUBLE

Antetokounmpo's rise to the top began with his outstanding rookie campaign, followed by a second season that saw improvement in many aspects of his game. By his fourth year Antetokounmpo was showing all the signs of a player ready to assume his role as one of the league's best. One of the things that he was able to do in his NBA senior year was record his first career triple-double. In a game during the 2016–2017 season (a breakout year for the star), Antetokounmpo scored 21 points, grabbed 11 rebounds (including nine on the defensive side of the ball), and had 10 assists to lead the Bucks to victory over Orlando.

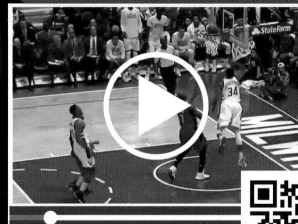

It took Antetokounmpo 251 games to record his first career triple-double, in a November 21, 2016, victory against the Orlando Magic.

Antetokounmpo handles the ball well enough to play any position on the court.

TEXT-DEPENDENT QUESTIONS

1. How many points did Antetokounmpo score in the 2019 NBA All-Star game as team captain for the East? How many points did he score in his first All-Star game appearance in 2017?

2. How many awards/recognitions did Antetokounmpo receive for the 2016–2017 season? What were they?

3. How many NBA games did Antetokounmpo play before recording his first triple-double?

 RESEARCH PROJECT

Antetokounmpo has earned several honors in his six-year career as a member of the Milwaukee Bucks. Taking the NBA draft classes from 2005 through 2018, determine which players from each class have earned multiple awards and honors including: MVP, MIP, All-Star, All-NBA, All-Offensive, All-Defensive, All-Star MVP, and Finals MVP. Determine which draft class produced the most players with multiple awards and honors and which draft class has produced the least number of players.

WORDS TO UNDERSTAND

assimilate: To absorb into the cultural tradition of a population or group

disparity: Lack of similarity or equality; inequality; difference

emigrate: To leave one country or region to settle in another

longevity: Length of service, tenure, etc.

CHAPTER 2

THE ROAD TO THE TOP

A DIFFERENT PATH

Giannis Antetokounmpo, born Ioannis Adetokunbo (the family name originating in Nigeria), was born in Athens, Greece, on December 6, 1994. His parents, Charles and Veronica, **emigrated** from Lagos to Athens, initially leaving their eldest son Francis (they later changed his name to the Greek "Andreas") behind with his grandparents, who later joined the family in Athens. Giannis's other brothers, Thanasis, Kostas, and Alexis, were all born in Athens. The family name "Adetokunbo" was changed to "Antetokounmpo" so that the family could better **assimilate** in their new country. Charles passed away in September of 2017.

Giannis dunks over his brother Thanasis while playing hoops in their Sepolia neighborhood in Athens, Greece.

Antetokounmpo comes from quite an athletic family. His father was a soccer player in Nigeria and his mother was a high jumper. Also benefitting from the familial athletic genes is his brother Andreas, who was also a Nigerian soccer player. Antetokounmpo played club basketball in Greece with two of his brothers: Thanasis, who is six feet seven inches (2.01 m), and was drafted by the New York Knicks in the 2014 NBA Draft (51st pick), and Kostas, who at six feet, ten inches (2.08 m) was taken with the 60th pick of the 2018 NBA draft by Philadelphia (Kostas is currently assigned to the Texas Legends, a developmental NBA G-League team affiliated with the Dallas Mavericks. He made his NBA debut with two games for Dallas in the 2018-2019 season).

Antetokounmpo's youngest brother, Alexis, a six foot seven inch (2.01 m) small forward, is a high school junior playing for Dominican High School (nickname: "Knights") in Whitefish Bay, Wisconsin, a suburb of Milwaukee.

Antetokounmpo's family settled in a small neighborhood located in Athens called Sepolia (taken from a Greek expression *"exo poleos"* or *"outside the city"*). It was in Sepolia that a thirteen-year-old Antetokounmpo began to develop the skills that would one day make him an NBA superstar. A scout from local club team Filathlitikos saw him play and immediately brought Antetokounmpo on as a member of their youth team in 2009. By 2011, he was elevated to the club's senior team, the equivalent of high school/college basketball in the U.S. Antetokounmpo was very popular in Greece for his ball-handling, defensive, and shooting skills.

By age eighteen, Antetokounmpo had grown to six feet nine inches (2.06 m) in height, but only weighed 196 pounds (88.9 kg). This **disparity** between his height and weight made him appear "super skinny" as some scouts remarked, making Antetokounmpo an unlikely high first round pick. He became eligible at age nineteen (2013) for the NBA draft and decided to try his luck playing overseas. His decision paid off as the Bucks took a chance on him by selecting him in the first round of the 2013 draft. Antetokounmpo's continued development from an extremely skinny kid to a full-size superstar in the making has rewarded the Bucks for gambling on the Greek kid with a hard to pronounce name!

NBA DRAFT DAY 2013 SIGNIFICANT ACCOUNTS

- Giannis Antetokounmpo was selected by the Milwaukee Bucks with the 15th pick in the first round of the 2013 NBA draft.

- The 2013 NBA draft was held at the Barclays Center in Brooklyn, New York, on June 27, 2013. The Barclays Center became the new permanent home for the NBA draft, which had been held at Madison Square Garden in Times Square, New York, for the previous 50 years (1960–2010).

- Antetokounmpo was the fifth forward selected in the 2013 NBA draft.

- Antetokounmpo was one of 21 forwards taken in the 2013 NBA draft (out of the 60 players drafted in rounds 1 and 2).

- The guard position was the largest group drafted in the 2013 draft (30), followed by forwards (21), and centers (nine).

- This was the first draft for the New Orleans Pelicans and last draft for the Charlotte Bobcats. New Orleans returned the name "Hornets" to Charlotte beginning with the 2013–2014 season. The Hornets moved from Charlotte to New Orleans in 2002.

- The sons of two former players were drafted in 2013, exactly 24 years after their fathers. Tim Hardaway Jr. (24th pick, drafted by the New York Knicks), the son of Tim Hardaway Sr., a five-time All-Star and All-NBA player for several teams (1989–2003), and Glen Rice, Jr. (35th pick, drafted by the Philadelphia 76ers), the son of Glen Rice Sr., a three-time All-Star and two-time All-NBA player with several NBA teams from 1989–2004. Rice Sr. was the fourth overall pick in the 1989 NBA draft, while Hardaway Sr. was the 14th pick in the same draft.

- Anthony Bennett (drafted by the Cleveland Cavaliers) was the number-one overall pick in the 2013 draft. He was born in Toronto, Ontario (Canada), and was the first Canadian-born player picked number one overall in an NBA draft.

- Antetokounmpo was one of 15 international players drafted in 2013.

Source: https://stats.nba.com/draft/history/?Season=2013–NBA draft information for 2013 NBA Draft.

Milwaukee took a chance drafting Antetokounmpo in the first round, but it has paid off better than could have been expected so far.

GROWING HIS GAME

Antetokounmpo did not attend high school growing up in Greece. Instead, he participated on semi-professional and professional basketball teams from age thirteen until the time he was an adult; in 2013, at the age of nineteen, he was he was drafted by the NBA Milwaukee Bucks. Alongside his brother Thanasis, Giannis played for a local basketball club, Filathlitikos, on its semi-professional C team for the 2011–2012 season, and its professional A2 team in 2012. Unfortunately, there are no stats available that show his progress from year to year as he was still young and developing his game with Filathlitikos.

Antetokounmpo played for a semi-pro team in Greece with his older brother Thanasis.

Antetokounmpo has also represented Greece in International Basketball Federation (FIBA) team events, both as a junior (under 20) and senior team member. He continued to participate on the country's FIBA national teams even after he was drafted by Milwaukee. Antetokounmpo's first international competition was the 2013 U-20 Euro Championship, played in Tallinn, Estonia (July 9–21, 2013). His squad finished fifth out of 16 teams that entered the tournament. Antetokounmpo scored 80 points in 10 games for an eight points per game average. Here are his stats for the 12-day event:

FIBA Junior Team (Greece)

YEAR	EVENT	G	FGM	FTM	REB	AST	STL	BLK	PTS	PPG
2013	U-20 Euro Champ	10	24	20	76	22	10	14	80	8.0
TOTAL		**10**	**24**	**20**	**76**	**22**	**10**	**14**	**80**	**8.0**

Antetokounmpo was also a member of the senior squad that competed in the following events:

- FIBA World Championship (2014)— held in Spain on August 30–September 14, 2014. His squad lost in a round of 16 match against Serbia in Madrid on September 7th, by the score of 90–72. The U.S. was the eventual champion, and Kyrie Irving of the Boston Celtics was named MVP for the tournament.

- FIBA EuroBasket (2015)—held in four countries (Croatia, France, Germany, and Latvia), September 5–20, 2015. Greece advanced to the quarterfinals, losing in a matchup against the eventual champion Spain, 73–71. As a result of his team's finish, Greece qualified for the World Olympic Qualifying Tournament.

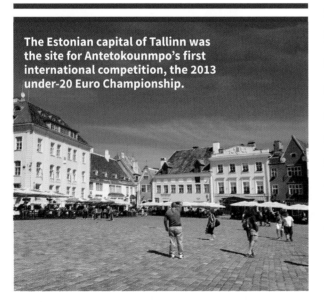

The Estonian capital of Tallinn was the site for Antetokounmpo's first international competition, the 2013 under-20 Euro Championship.

- World Olympic Qualifying Tournament (2016)—Held in Turin, Italy, from July

4–9, 2016. Greece finished third, winning the bronze medal for its group, but failed to qualify for the 2016 Rio de Janeiro (Brazil) Summer Olympics. Antetokounmpo led all players in blocks per game (2.0) and free throw percentage (100 percent). His brother Thanasis, also a member of Greece's national team, was third in blocks with 1.3 a game.

Here are his stats for these three senior events he participated in:

FIBA Senior Team (Greece)

YEAR	EVENT	G	FGM	FTM	REB	AST	STL	BLK	PTS	PPG
2014	FIBA World Cup	6	11	15	26	2	4	2	38	6.3
2015	FIBA EuroBasket	8	30	8	55	9	2	7	78	9.8
2016	Olympic Qualifier	3	16	9	17	6	2	6	46	15.3
TOTAL		17	57	32	98	17	8	15	162	9.5

PLAYER COMPARISON: ANTETOKOUNMPO TO NOWITZKI

A player that Antetokounmpo looks up to and admires is Dirk Nowitzki of the Dallas Mavericks. Nowitzki has played his entire career in Dallas and has been a league MVP, NBA Finals MVP, and NBA Champion. Nowitzki started his career in much the same way that Antetokounmpo started his. He was known as the "German Wunderkind" playing in his native Würzburg, Germany. Nowitzki spent time developing into an NBA player playing on local club teams and, when the time came, passed on college and entered the 1998 NBA draft (he was the ninth pick of the draft by Milwaukee, and was traded to Dallas).

ONE FOREIGN-BORN SUPERSTAR DISCUSSES THE POTENTIAL OF ANOTHER

Dirk Nowitzki is, arguably, the greatest foreign-born star to have ever played in the NBA. His 21 seasons with the Dallas Mavericks are an NBA record for most years with one franchise. He also ranks at the top of the all-time list for career **longevity**, tied with Kevin Garnett, Robert Parrish, Kevin Willis, and Vince Carter. Nowitzki has won an NBA championship (and the NBA Finals MVP in 2011) and has been named league MVP in 2007. He is a 14-time All-Star and was named All-NBA 12 times. These accomplishments are what Antetokounmpo aspires to, so much so that he selected Nowitzki to be on his team for the 2019 All-Star game as team captain. The admiration between these players is mutual!

These career highlights show why Antetokounmpo considers Dirk Nowitzki to be such a great player.

Antetokounmpo grew up watching and admiring Dallas Maverick superstar Dirk Nowitzki, the NBA's most successful international player ever.

It is interesting to look at the careers of these two big men—Nowitzki, who stands at 7 feet tall (2.13 m), has a style and approach to the game that is very similar to Antetokounmpo's. A look at their rookie and 2018–2019 seasons, as well as a comparison of their first six NBA seasons, seems to indicate great things for the Greek Freak, when compared to his hero, the German Wunderkind:

Rookie Season

Season	Player	Tm	G	FG%	REB	AST	STL	BLK	PTS	PPG	RPG	APG
2013–14	Antetokounmpo	MIL	77	41.4%	339	150	60	61	525	6.8	4.4	1.9
1999–00	Nowitzki	DAL	47	40.5%	162	47	29	27	385	8.2	3.4	1.0

Nowitzki was no longer a starter for the Dallas Mavericks during the 2018–2019 season and appeared in only a few games while Antetokounmpo started all the games he played in for the Milwaukee Bucks. Here are their stats as they compare (up to the 2019 All-Star break):

2018–2019 Season

Player	G	FG%	REB	AST	STL	BLK	PTS	PPG	RPG	APG
Antetokounmpo	72	57.8	898	424	73	110	1,994	27.7	12.5	5.9
Nowitzki	51	35.9	158	35	9	18	373	7.3	3.1	0.7

Nowitzki parades the NBA championship trophy through Dallas after the Mavericks won the league title in 2011.

Career (Comparison through first six seasons)

Season	Player	G	FG%	REB	AST	STL	BLK	PTS	PPG	RPG	APG
2013-19	*Antetokounmpo*	*465*	*52.1*	*3,844*	*1,921*	*559*	*626*	*8,745*	*18.8*	*8.3*	*4.1*
1998-2019	Nowitzki	444	46.4	3,664	1,055	457	459	9,074	20.4	8.3	2.4

The numbers show that through a very similar number of games played, Antetokounmpo stacks up to the sure-fire Hall of Famer that he idolized. Nowitzki was the slightly better scorer, but Antetokounmpo has superior numbers in every other category, especially on the defensive end.

TEXT-DEPENDENT QUESTIONS

1. What year was Antetokounmpo drafted? What was his draft selection number? What team drafted him?

2. What country are his parents from? In what country was he born?

3. How many brothers does he have? What sport did his oldest brother play? In what country?

RESEARCH PROJECT

Antetokounmpo announced, just prior to the 2019 NBA All-Star game, that he would play for his native Greece in the 2019 FIBA World Basketball Championship, known as the Basketball World Cup. Looking at the 32 participating teams (other than the United States), find the NBA players that participated in the event. Include the name of the team the player was on in the 2018–2019 NBA season and the country he represented.

WORDS TO UNDERSTAND

economic: Pertaining to the production, distribution, and use of income, wealth, and commodities

prowess: Exceptional or superior ability, skill, or strength

stipend: A fixed or regular amount of money paid as a salary or allowance

tentative: Unsure; uncertain; not definite or positive; hesitant

CHAPTER 3

ON THE COURT

COMING TO AMERICA

Life for Antetokounmpo was anything but ideal growing up. He wasn't considered a citizen of Greece until he reached the age of eighteen, making it difficult for him to enjoy many aspects of Greek life. Antetokounmpo's family also had a tough time finding steady work, as the country was experiencing an **economic** downturn. This meant that every member of the Antetokounmpo family had to pitch in to help out the family financially. They did every type of job imaginable, including picking oranges on a local farm. Antetokounmpo also worked with his older brother, Thanasis, to sell whatever they could get their hands on so that they could help feed his large family.

As Antetokounmpo's interest in basketball grew, he was able to secure a small **stipend** from Filathlitikos to allow him to focus on basketball and take care of his family. When he turned nineteen, he **tentatively** accepted a

Antetokounmpo turned down a contract to play in Spain when the Bucks drafted him.

contract to play professional basketball in Spain for CAI Zaragoza for 400,000 euros ($453,304) per year. Before he could put a uniform on for the team, he was drafted by the Bucks and instead came to America to begin his NBA journey.

ON THE COURT ACCOMPLISHMENTS

Antetokounmpo grew from six feet nine inches (2.06 m) to six feet eleven inches (2.11 m) by his second year in the league. He has a wingspan (fingertip to fingertip with arms spread wide) of seven feet three inches (2.21 m). Antetokounmpo's growth spurt, coupled with his reach, makes him uniquely designed to cause trouble on both the offensive and defensive sides of the basketball court. This has suited him well, as he has improved every year he has been in the NBA, going from a scoring average in his rookie year of 6.8 points per game (ppg) to more than 26 ppg midway through the 2018–2019 NBA season.

Antetokounmpo is the only player in NBA history to finish a season ranked 20th or higher in blocks, steals, assists, rebounds, and total points scored. He has been in the focus of discussion as a possible league MVP since the 2016–2017 season, competing with the likes of Russell Westbrook (Oklahoma City Thunder), James Harden (Houston Rockets), Stephen Curry (Golden State Warriors), Anthony Davis (New Orleans Pelicans), and LeBron James (Los Angeles Lakers).

Antetokounmpo (#34), seen here against Utah in 2015, is the offensive leader on the floor for the Bucks.

GIANNIS ANTETOKOUNMPO

FORWARD / GUARD

- Date of birth: December 6, 1994

- Height: six feet eleven inches (2.11 m); Weight: Approx. 242 pounds (109 kg)

- Drafted in the first round in 2013 (15th pick overall) by the Milwaukee Bucks

- All-NBA First Team (2019)

- Named to the NBA All-Defensive First Team (2019)

- Named NBA Most Valuable Player (2019)

- Named NBA Most Improved Player in the 2016–2017 season

- Named to three All-Star games (2017–2019), including being named team captain of the Eastern Conference squad in 2019

- Two-time All-NBA Second Team selection (2017, 2018)

- Named to the NBA All-Defensive Second Team (2017)

CAREER TOTALS

Here are the career, playoff, and all-star game numbers Antetokounmpo has put up through the 2018–2019 NBA season:

SEASON	TM	G	FGM	FG%	FTM	FT%	REB	AST	STL	BLK	PTS	PPG
2013–14	MIL	77	173	41.4%	138	68.3%	339	150	60	61	525	6.8
2014–15	MIL	81	383	49.1%	257	74.1%	542	207	73	85	1030	12.7
2015–16	MIL	80	513	50.6%	296	72.4%	612	345	94	113	1350	16.9
2016–17	MIL	80	656	52.1%	471	77.0%	700	434	131	151	1832	22.9
2017–18	MIL	75	742	52.9%	487	76.0%	753	361	109	106	2014	26.9
2018–19	MIL	72	721	57.8	500	72.9	898	424	73	110	1994	27.7
TOTAL		465	3,188	52.1	2,149	74.2	3,824	1,921	559	626	8745	18.8

The 2016–2017 season was the first time Antetokounmpo averaged 20 points or more a game. It was the beginning of his climb to the level of those players considered as the best in the league. It was also the season when Antetokounmpo served notice to the rest of the league that he was a serious player who was continuing to develop and grow, and that his Milwaukee Bucks were a team that he would put on his shoulders, if necessary, to carry them to a championship.

Antetokounmpo defends the rim against Marcin Gortat of Washington.

PLAYOFF TOTALS

Through the 2019 postseason, Antetokounmpo has appeared in 34 playoff games in his career with the Milwaukee Bucks. His playoff appearances have led to his scoring a total of 781 points, for an average of 23 points per game. Antetokounmpo's point production has increased in each of the seasons that he has appeared in the playoffs (2015, 69 points; 2017, 149 points; 2018, 180 points; 2019, 383 points). Additionally, he has averaged 10.3 rebounds and 4.6 assists per game in the 34 appearances, has made 43 steals, and pulled down 350 rebounds, including 283 defensive boards. Antetokounmpo has made 50.2% of his field goals attempted and nearly a third (32.5%) of his three-point attempts.

The Bucks posted the best record in the NBA during the 2018–2019 season. This was due largely to Antetokounmpo's 27.7 point per game average and ability to control games and assert his will on opponents. He led the Bucks on a winning run that they have not experienced since the 2000–2001 season, which was the last time the team won at least 50 games.

Here are his performance statistics for his 34 playoff games:

SEASON	TM	G	FGM	FG%	FTM	FT%	REB	AST	STL	BLK	PTS	PPG
2014–15	MIL	6	26	36.6%	17	73.9%	42	42	16	3	69	11.5
2016–17	MIL	6	60	53.6%	25	54.3%	57	57	24	13	149	24.8
2017–18	MIL	7	69	57.0%	38	69.1%	67	67	44	10	180	25.7
2018–19	MIL	15	129	49.2%	107	63.7%	184	73	17	30	383	25.5
TOTAL		34	284	50.2%	187	64.0%	350	157	43	55	781	23.0

ALL-STAR GAMES TOTALS

Antetokounmpo was selected to appear in three consecutive All-Star games from 2016 to 2019. For each of his all-star appearances he has been selected as a starter. He has a 28.0 point per appearance average and led all All-Stars in the 2019 game in scoring, with 38 points. Additionally, Antetokounmpo was the second-highest recipient of votes, behind LeBron James of the Los Angeles Lakers. Since he received the most votes for the Eastern Conference, he was named team captain.

Here are his All-Star game scoring totals (through 2019):

SEASON	TM	G	FGM	FG%	REB	AST	STL	BLK	PTS	PPG
2016–17	MIL	1	14	82.4%	6	1	3	1	30	30.0
2017–18	MIL	1	6	42.9%	7	2	0	0	16	16.0
2018–19	MIL	1	17	73.9%	11	5	1	0	38	38.0
TOTAL		3	37	68.5%	24	8	4	1	84	28.0

Antetokounmpo shared captain's duties at the 2019 NBA All-Star game with LeBron James of the Los Angeles Lakers.

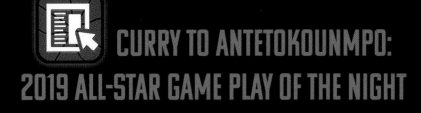

CURRY TO ANTETOKOUNMPO:
2019 ALL-STAR GAME PLAY OF THE NIGHT

Antetokounmpo served notice to the rest of the NBA with his 38 point, 11 rebound performance (his first All-Star game double-double) in the 2019 NBA All-Star game. His scoring **prowess** led to several highlight-worthy dunks that punctuated his night. One of his highlight dunks certainly qualified as the play of the game. On a transition play against Team LeBron, Golden State Warriors' guard Stephen Curry bounced a pass on the hardwood that went high above the rim; Antetokounmpo soared above the rim and with his right hand, brought the ball down through the rim with authority for a thrilling play.

Antetokounmpo and Curry collaborate on a dunk for the ages in the 2019 NBA All-Star game.

RANKING ANTETOKOUNMPO

Antetokounmpo's career compares favorably to that of the other members of the 2013–2014 All-Rookie team, to which he was also named (to the second team). When comparing his six-year career with that of these players, here is how he stacks up:

Pk	Player	Draft Team	Current Team	Yrs	G	PTS	REB	AST	PPG
15	G. Antetokounmpo	MIL	MIL	6	465	8,745	3,844	1,921	18.8
2	Victor Oladipo	ORL	IND	6	402	7,028	1,859	1,589	17.5
24	Tim Hardaway Jr.	NYK	DAL	6	403	5,267	1,033	740	13.1
12	Steven Adams	OKC	OKC	6	467	4,507	3,446	469	9.7
13	Kelly Olynyk	BOS	MIA	6	433	4,287	2116	818	9.9
22	Mason Plumlee	BYN	DEN	6	471	3,989	2,977	1,029	8.5
9	Trey Burke	UTH	DAL	6	361	3,924	741	1,301	10.9
21	Gorgui Dieng	MIN	MIN	6	452	3,594	2,812	629	8.0
11	M. Carter-Williams*	PHI	ORL	6	315	3,426	1,427	1,463	10.9
4	Cody Zeller	CHA	CHA	6	361	2,969	2,085	495	8.2

*Was named Rookie of the Year for the 2013–2014 NBA season.

The Pacers' Victor Oladipo is the only other player in Antetokounmpo's rookie class to also have at least 1,500 rebounds and 1,500 assists.

Antetokounmpo leads his nine fellow 2014 all-rookie members in points per game, total points scored, rebounds, and assists, although Michael Carter-Williams has more assists per games played. Antetokounmpo is one of two players from the 2014 All-Rookie team (along with Victor Oladipo of the Indiana Pacers) to be named to an All-Star team (both players were named Most Improved Player: Antetokounmpo in 2017 and Oladipo in 2018).

Former 76er Michael Carter-Williams (#1) was the Rookie of the Year from Antetokounmpo's draft class, but injuries have stalled his once-bright career.

TEXT-DEPENDENT QUESTIONS

1. How many All-Star appearances has Antetokounmpo made through the 2018–2019 season? How many points did he score in the 2019 All-Star game?

2. How many playoff games has he played in his NBA career through the 2017–2018 season?

3. What year did Antetokounmpo appear in his first NBA All-Star game?

RESEARCH PROJECT

Antetokounmpo is a foreign-born basketball sensation who went straight to the NBA at age nineteen without ever stepping on a college campus. He is one of several foreign-born players who has found success in the NBA and did not take the traditional route of high school stardom and college play to make it to the professional level. Looking at the foreign players who have come in the league since 2000, find at least 10 players that attended college (either in the U.S. or abroad) before entering the NBA draft, and 10 players who, like Antetokounmpo, played either professionally overseas or for a club team in their country. For those who went to college, list the player, the school they attended, the year(s) they attended, and the year they were drafted into the NBA. For those players who did not attend college, again, list the player, the professional club or team they played for, and the year they entered the draft.

 WORDS TO UNDERSTAND

aver: To assert or affirm with confidence; declare in a positive or peremptory manner

dextrous: Skillful or adroit in the use of the hands or body

extolled: Highly praised; lauded

perennial: Lasting for an indefinitely long time; enduring

CHAPTER 4

WORDS COUNT

When the time comes to address the media before or after a game, players either retreat to the comfort of traditional phrases that avoid controversy (Cliché City), or they speak their mind with refreshing candor (Quote Machine).

Here are 10 quotes, compiled in part from the website brainyquote.com, with some insight as to the context of what Antetokounmpo was talking about or referencing:

"If you are going to do something, you have to do it for yourself, and that's what I try to do. I try to be authentic and try to be original, so that's what I try to be. A lot of people try to build big brands but have received bad advice, and they don't try to be authentic and real with themselves."

Antetokounmpo has a much lower profile than other NBA stars like fellow 2019 NBA MVP candidate and 2018 MVP James Harden.

Antetokounmpo, a young man in his early twenties, is wise beyond his years. His quote **avers** his opinion that the best approach to life is staying true to your own set of values, instead of trying to be something you are not. Antetokounmpo has become a superstar in the NBA, not by trying to be like other stars in the league, but by playing the game his way. He is perhaps the most original star in the NBA and yet one of the less **extolled** when compared to the likes of Stephen Curry, LeBron James, Russell Westbrook, James Harden, and Kevin Durant. Antetokounmpo knows that as long as he keeps doing things as he was raised to do them, he will always be the original Giannis Antetokounmpo.

Rating: Quote Machine

"It's my nature to be fearless."

Antetokounmpo plays the game with a natural feel for the basketball and is surprisingly **dexterous** for a man who stands six feet eleven inches (2.11 m). He is listed as a guard and forward, with the ability to jump center on occasion when his team needs him to play the big man role. Antetokounmpo has abundant natural talent and ability, and because of it, he has no fear of putting his body at risk to make a play for the Bucks. This sense of fearlessness is something he developed growing up with four other siblings, two of which also played at the professional level, as well as having been raised by immigrant parents with no national identity until he reached the age of eighteen. Fearlessness has allowed Antetokounmpo to take chances and believe in his ability to create his own success. **Rating: Quote Machine**

"Just growing up and going through life and how tough life was for me and my family, I'm always going to stay humble."

Antetokounmpo's humility comes from his parents, Charles and Veronica Antetokounmpo. Although his father passed away in 2017, Antetokounmpo was there to provide support for his family, despite the struggles they had living in a new country with a struggling economy and little work available to immigrants. Antetokounmpo has picked oranges, sold small items, and done whatever he needed to do to help out his family financially and feed himself. Throughout all of these difficulties, he had the love and support of his parents and brothers, who allowed him to play basketball and develop the skills he would need to attract the attention of NBA scouts and eventually sign a $100 million contract extension with the Milwaukee Bucks. Though his journey is unique, many NBA players succeed by overcoming difficult circumstances, and we have heard this quote many times before. Despite his success, Antetokounmpo has remained very humble and appreciative of the opportunities that he has been given, which have allowed him to take care of his family. **Rating: Cliché City**

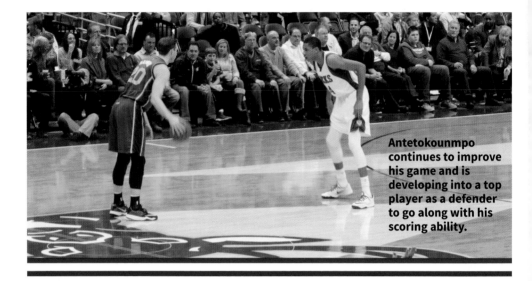

Antetokounmpo continues to improve his game and is developing into a top player as a defender to go along with his scoring ability.

> "I'm gonna have some nights when it's not gonna come. But if you keep playing natural, it's just gonna come. I'm gonna keep getting better, keep getting better, and one day, everything's gonna pay off."

Antetokounmpo is still developing as a player. As he continues to develop and get better from season to season, he knows that he is likely to turn in performances that are less than what has become expected of him. Recognizing that this may happen, Antetokounmpo knows that as long as he continues to work hard, listen to his coaches, and play naturally, that he will achieve success and have not just a good—but a great—NBA career.

Rating: Quote Machine

FLY THE FRIENDLY SKIES WITH ANTETOKOUNMPO

Antetokounmpo has become a spokesperson of a different sort these days. His fame as an NBA player has made him a popular hero in his home country of Greece. This fame has translated into his completing a safety video for the Greek national airline, Aegean Airline. The video shows flight attendants narrating the standard airline safety activities we all see when flying on the plane, with Antetokounmpo demonstrating each of them. This tongue-in-cheek approach to airline safety will certainly catch the attention of Greek passengers, or fans of the game who fly the friendly skies of Greek airline Aegean.

Greece's Aegean Airline's newest spokesperson—and national hero—Giannis Antetokounmpo of the Milwaukee Bucks, commands your full attention during these important airline safety tips.

> "We loved our dad. My mom loved her husband. But at the end of the day, I think, he did what he was supposed to do in this world. He had five kids and raised us right. That's the most important thing."

There is considerable speculation that Antetokounmpo may be lured to Golden State to play with Stephen Curry and the Warriors in 2021, although the Greek Freak has insisted that he wants to win a championship in Milwaukee.

Antetokounmpo's father, Charles, died in September of 2017. He was the head of the family and did everything he could to make a better life for his wife Veronica and five sons. Charles worked hard and instilled a sense of hard work, commitment, humility, and pride in his children. He was able to live long enough to move to Wisconsin with his son and see him grow from a skinny six feet nine inch- (2.06 m) tall, nineteen-year-old kid to a confident young man and leader of the Milwaukee Bucks. Charles was also able to (briefly) reap the rewards of his son's success. What Charles passed on to his son was worth more than all of the money he has and will earn playing basketball. What he passed on was what it means to be a man and a responsible one at that.

Rating: Quote Machine

Antetokounmpo's eye-opening performance at the 2019 NBA All-Star game (where he led all players with 38 points and 11 rebounds) has fueled a lot of speculation about his future when his contract

> **"My goal is to win in Milwaukee, bring a championship in the city, and make the team a lot better. So I would never leave for LA."**

is up in 2021. One such rumor has Antetokounmpo going from Milwaukee to Golden State to play alongside Stephen Curry, DeMarcus Cousins, and Draymond Green (and maybe Kevin Durant). Such a team would be nearly unstoppable in the NBA. Antetokounmpo says he enjoys living in Milwaukee and is grateful for the opportunity that the team has given him to play. His goal is to help lead the Bucks to their first NBA championship in almost 50 years and to make the team a **perennial** title contender. Antetokounmpo doesn't see himself leaving Milwaukee for the riches that can be found in Los Angeles or New York. Only time will tell what he will decide.

Rating: Quote Machine

> **"I want to become one of the best players, so if you want to be one the best, you have to elevate all aspects of your game."**

The only player to complete an NBA season in the top 20 in all five major statistical categories (rebounds, points, steals, blocks, assists) understands that to be the best, you have to be the best on both sides of the ball. He just didn't express it in a particularly original way in this

Basketball Hall of Fame point guard Jason Kidd, who coached Giannis in Milwaukee, compared Antetokounmpo's game to that of Kidd's former teammate, Dirk Nowitzki.

quote. Antetokounmpo has been named to the All-NBA second team in the 2016–2017 and 2017–2018 seasons and All-Defensive second team in 2016–2017. You don't acquire those honors without doing the work to elevate your game at all levels, both on offense and defense. Antetokounmpo sees himself not just as the best player on the Milwaukee Bucks or the best player in the Central division of the Eastern Conference, but the best player in the entire NBA. Being named a team captain in the 2019 All-Star game means that he is starting to receive the recognition he deserves as one of the best players.

Rating: Cliché City

"The things that Dirk has done for this league and for the Dallas Mavericks, it's unbelievable. And Coach Kidd was a teammate of Dirk, so for Jason Kidd to compare me with Dirk Nowitzki, it feels nice. It's a nice compliment."

Antetokounmpo is an absolute fan of Dirk Nowitzki of the Dallas Mavericks. He considers it a high compliment that his former coach, Hall-of-Famer Jason Kidd, who played four seasons with Nowitzki, compared him to his idol. Everything about Antetokounmpo's game is similar to the way Nowitzki plays. He knows that if that is the standard he is being compared with as a player, this means he must be doing something right in trying to mold himself after a future Hall of Fame member. Antetokounmpo presumably wants everything about his career to be like Nowitzki's career, like winning an NBA championship (or several championships), being named MVP, and eventually being selected to join the NBA Hall of Fame in Springfield, Massachusetts. **Rating: Quote Machine**

> **"Because my parents were illegal, they couldn't trust anybody. They were always nervous. A neighbor could be like, 'These people are making too much noise, their children are making too much noise,' and the cops could knock at our door and ask for our papers, and that's it. It's that simple. So you're always a little closed."**

Times were difficult for the Antetokounmpo family living as immigrants in Greece. Not having the proper documentation as citizens made it difficult for them to become close to many people in their community, for fear of being found out as undocumented immigrants. This created a lot of stress and tension for the family, for fear of being reported as illegal and possibly sent back to their native Nigeria, a country that was as foreign to the Antetokounmpo brothers as Greece was to their parents. As the boys took up the game of basketball and became good at it, representing the country internationally, this nervousness went away and now Antetokounmpo considers Greece both his country of origin and home.

Rating: Quote Machine

"What's the reason I'm playing basketball? I do it because I love it, I do it because of my family, and that's it. I don't do it because of the money. I don't do it because of the fame. I just do it because I love it, and I do it for my family because my family enjoys it."

Antetokounmpo's love of the game is evident every time he is out on the court.

Antetokounmpo first began playing basketball in 2007, in his early teens. The game of basketball was the one place he could go to get away from the stress of his living situation. Antetokounmpo developed a genuine love for the game and as he continued to grow, his game got better. Obviously, if it weren't for basketball, he may never have had the opportunity to improve the life of his family and ease their financial burdens. Antetokounmpo's motivation for playing basketball, as he tells it, does not come from the money he makes, although he does make a lot of money playing the game. It comes from his passion for playing, the challenge of getting better each season, and the idea of being considered as one of the best players in the game. **Rating: Quote Machine**

TEXT-DEPENDENT QUESTIONS

1. What are the names of Antetokounmpo's mother and father? What year did his father pass away?

2. How tall is Antetokounmpo (in feet and meters)?

3. What former Dallas Maverick player (and former teammate of Dirk Nowitzki) coached Antetokounmpo in Milwaukee?

 **RESEARCH PROJECT**

Antetokounmpo is one of three brothers who have been drafted into the NBA (his brother Thanasis was drafted in 2014 with the 51st overall pick by the New York Knicks while brother Kostas was taken by the Philadelphia 76ers in the 2018 draft with the last pick). They are not the only brothers who have been drafted over the years and whose paths have crossed in the NBA. Look at the NBA over its entire history to find a pair (or more) of brothers who were drafted within five years of each other. List the brothers, the year(s) they played, when they were drafted, and the name of the team(s) that drafted them.

WORDS TO UNDERSTAND

compulsory: Required; mandatory; obligatory

immigrant: A person who migrates to another country, usually for permanent residence

resurgent: Rising or tending to rise again; reviving; renascent

trinkets: Anything of trivial value

CHAPTER 5

OFF THE COURT

ANTETOKOUNMPO'S EDUCATION

Antetokounmpo's formal education came mostly from the time he spent at the Zografou indoor arena in Athens. It was there that he and his brother Thanasis were accepted and taught the game of basketball, despite the family's lack of funds, and he spent much of his time selling **trinkets** on the streets have enough money to eat. It was difficult for the Antetokounmpo brothers growing up as undocumented persons living in the country of their birth. Their status as **immigrants** made it difficult for them to enjoy basic freedoms other native-born Greeks enjoyed, such as attending school and receiving a formal education.

Since developing into a top pick and earning a tremendous salary for his basketball talent, Antetokounmpo has been able to move his family to the U.S.

Antetokounmpo and his brothers sold all sorts of trinkets and odds and ends on the street to help make ends meet for their family.

and provide opportunities for his younger brothers, Kostas and Alexis. Alexis attended Dominican High School in Whitefish Bay, Wisconsin, and Kostas studied at the University of Dayton (nickname: "Flyers") in Dayton, Ohio. Alexis is a high school junior who led his Dominican Knights team to a state championship and is being heralded as a college prospect. He has received interest from the in-state schools of the University of Wisconsin at Green Bay (nickname: "Phoenix") and the University of Wisconsin at Madison (nickname: "Badgers").

ANTETOKOUNMPO AT HOME

Antetokounmpo was born and raised in Athens, Greece, as the son of an immigrant family from Lagos, Nigeria. He was not officially recognized as a Greek citizen until just after he turned eighteen, leaving him without a national identity for most of his childhood. Antetokounmpo and his brother Thanasis helped his struggling family make ends meet by peddling odds and ends they would find or acquire, and it was this experience that has helped shape his life, as well as mold his understanding about the importance of family.

Antetokounmpo's rookie contract gave him a tremendous amount of financial freedom that he had not had before. It took him some time to adjust to having money, however. Antetokounmpo once had to walk to a game in Milwaukee, after he sent every penny of his paycheck to his family in Athens, leaving him without enough money to even take a taxi.

Eventually, with the money he earned from his rookie contract with the Bucks, Antetokounmpo was able to move his entire family from Athens to the United States (except for brother Andreas, who remained in Greece to continue his professional soccer career). He purchased his first home in 2018 in the Milwaukee suburb of River Hills, located north of the city. The home, which Antetokounmpo purchased for $1.8 million, is more than spacious enough for the entire Antetokounmpo clan, and is a far cry from the home he knew while struggling to make ends meet for his family in Sepolia (Athens).

It is a five-bedroom, seven-and-a-half-bathroom home that features a home theater (presumably for the Antetokounmpo family to use to watch all of his spectacular dunks) and an in-ground swimming pool. The home was purchased by Antetokounmpo from a former Bucks teammate, Mirza Teletovic. Teletovic is also a foreign-national player (from Bosnia and Herzegovina) who played six seasons in the NBA, the last two with the Bucks (and who now serves as president of the Bosnian Basketball Federation). The home also features a guest house, a wine cellar, and even a workshop for him to work on other crafts (outside of basketball).

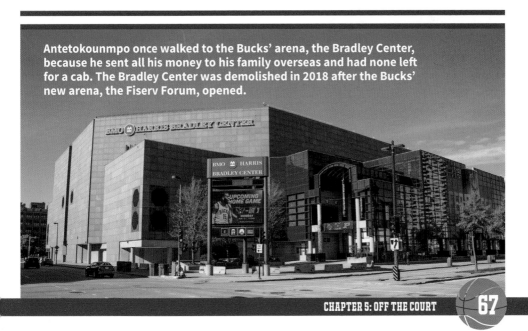

Antetokounmpo once walked to the Bucks' arena, the Bradley Center, because he sent all his money to his family overseas and had none left for a cab. The Bradley Center was demolished in 2018 after the Bucks' new arena, the Fiserv Forum, opened.

GIVING BACK TO THE COMMUNITY

Perhaps because of his upbringing and the way his family struggled as foreigners in a foreign land, Antetokounmpo has been a huge supporter of efforts to support his community and help those less fortunate than him. He has become a big part of the Milwaukee community, which, like the country of Greece, has adopted him as a favorite son. His engagement with the city is significant when considering the fact that Milwaukee, a small market for

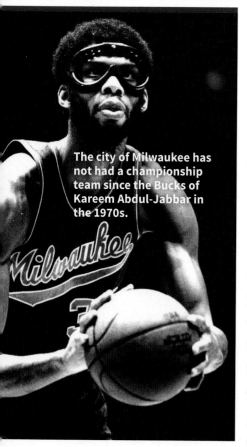

The city of Milwaukee has not had a championship team since the Bucks of Kareem Abdul-Jabbar in the 1970s.

professional sports leagues, was home to sports stars like Hank Aaron and Kareem Abdul-Jabbar, respective Hall-of-Famers in baseball and basketball who both won championships in Milwaukee. Championship-caliber athletes do not come along in Milwaukee very often. There is a sense of renewed pride and hope that Antetokounmpo will be able to bring championship glory to a city that has not seen a championship since the Bucks won one in 1971.

Antetokounmpo makes himself available for many causes, particularly those that deal with youth and refugees (as he and his family once were). This includes the Leukemia & Lymphoma Society, Milwaukee-area charities that support food banks and provide meals to hungry families (another issue that is important and personal to him), and the MACC Fund Research Center (MACC stands for Midwest Athletes Against Childhood Cancer, a Milwaukee-based charity that addresses the issue of childhood cancer).

Antetokounmpo likes to give personally to youth who are ailing or otherwise experiencing financial difficulties. One instance of his generosity involved a Greek youth, fifteen-year-old Dimitris Zamanis, who suffers from a disease called aplastic anemia. It is a condition where the body does not produce enough red blood cells, which are necessary for carrying oxygen to tissues in the body and removing carbon dioxide, which can result in the poisoning of the body. Because of the disease, Zamanis had to give up on his dream of playing basketball. Through the Make-A-Wish Foundation, Zamanis, his brother, and mother were able to travel from Greece to Milwaukee where he met in person his hero, Antetokounmpo. The experience was described by Zamanis as "the best day of his life."

THE BROTHERS ANTETOKOUNMPO'S STINT IN THE GREEK ARMY

As a citizen of Greece, Antetokounmpo is required to complete what is known as compulsory military service. This requirement applies to all male Greek citizens once they turn eighteen. He, and his older brother Thanasis, were no exception to the rule, even though they were spending time as citizens living abroad and playing basketball. The brothers reported in July 2016 to their duties in the Greek army's communication division for three months. The required service usually last nine months; he and Thanasis were able to receive a deferment from serving the remaining six months while they continue their hoop dreams.

The Bucks and Make-A-Wish partnered to grant Dimitris Zamanis, a fifteen-year-old from Greece who is living with aplastic anemia, his wish to meet and spend time with his idol, Giannis Antetokounmpo.

MARKETING ANTETOKOUNMPO

Antetokounmpo is represented by the Octagon sports agency, the same agency that represents Golden State Warriors star guard Stephen Curry. His agent is Alex Saratsis, who is a Senior Director at Chicago-based Octagon and is its Director of Basketball. Octagon bills itself as the largest sports and entertainment agency in the world. Saratsis also represents Kostas Antetokounmpo of the Dallas Mavericks and, coincidentally, Steph Curry's brother, Seth, of the Portland Trailblazers.

Some of the brands that Antetokounmpo has been associated with include:

- Tissot
- Bank of Montreal
- Nike

- Aegean Airlines (the national airline of Greece)

Just prior to the 2019 All-Star game (and perhaps as a result of his being named a team captain, alongside LeBron James), Antetokounmpo signed a deal with Metro by T-Mobile. The deal, for which financial terms have not been

Antetokounmpo shares an agent with Golden State's Stephen Curry.

disclosed, will involve his being a spokesperson for the brand on various types of platforms, such as print, multimedia and video.

Antetokounmpo's partnership with Nike has resulted in the development of his own signature shoe. Released in the autumn of 2018, the Greek Freak 1 is the first shoe that was developed for Antetokounmpo. Additionally, his deal with Nike is up for renewal in 2019. He currently makes $25,000 a year from the deal; the rumor is that Antetokounmpo's new deal will be near $50 million, which is more in line with his rise in stardom. His growing fame on the court has translated into more opportunities for him to become a spokesperson and represent various brands.

SALARY INFORMATION

In 2013, Antetokounmpo signed his rookie contract with the Bucks worth $8.6 million over a four-year period. This kept him with the team through the 2016–2017 season. Here is a breakdown of Antetokounmpo's salary earnings since his rookie contract in 2013:

Season	Team	Salary
2013-14	Milwaukee Bucks	$ 1,792,560
2014-15	Milwaukee Bucks	$ 1,873,200
2015-16	Milwaukee Bucks	$ 1,953,960
2016-17	Milwaukee Bucks	$ 2,995,421
TOTAL		**$ 8,615,141**

Antetokounmpo's next deal with giant sports apparel manufacturer Nike is projected to be worth almost $50 million per year.

As Antetokounmpo began to assume the leadership role for the **resurgent** Bucks team, the ownership group (which includes Green Bay Packers quarterback Aaron Rodgers, who owns a small percentage of the team) did everything they could to keep him from going to a larger market team, such as New York (Knicks or Nets) or Los Angeles (Lakers or Clippers).

The team exercised an option in 2016–2017 to keep Antetokounmpo in Milwaukee. A new four-year deal was negotiated between Antetokounmpo and the team on September 20, 2016, worth exactly $100 million.

Season	Team	Salary
2017-18	Milwaukee Bucks	$ 22,471,910
2018-19	Milwaukee Bucks	$ 24,157,304
2019-20	Milwaukee Bucks	$ 25,842,696
2020-21	Milwaukee Bucks	$ 27,528,090
TOTAL		**$100,000,000**

A skinny immigrant kid from the streets of Athens that sold small items to tourists just to feed his family has grown into a man who is changing the NBA.

Expectations are high in Milwaukee that as long as Antetokounmpo remains in a Bucks uniform, their prospects for an NBA championship run high. His skills are on par with (and in many respects above) those of some of the game's best players. Antetokounmpo is a welcome change from the type of superstar we have grown used to seeing. He brings his big hands (measuring one foot, or 0.30 m in length), big smile, big heart, and newfound love for smoothies with him to the court every night. Watching him play gives you a sense that even greater things are yet to come for the Greek Freak!

TEXT-DEPENDENT QUESTIONS

1. When did the Milwaukee Bucks last win an NBA championship?
2. Who represents Antetokounmpo as an agent? What other player does his agent's group represent?
3. What was the value of the contract extension he signed in 2016, and for how many years?

RESEARCH PROJECT

Antetokounmpo is one of a handful of NBA players with contracts that are valued at $100 million or more. Research and make a list of these players and rank them in order of average salary per year to determine which player makes the highest average annual salary. Do further research to determine if the player making the most per year is the highest-paid NBA player in the history

assist: a pass that directly leads to a teammate making a basket.

blocked shot: when a defensive player stops a shot at the basket by hitting the ball away.

center: a player whose main job is to score near the basket and win offensive and defensive rebounds. Centers are usually the tallest players on the court, and the best are able to move with speed and agility.

double dribble: when a player dribbles the ball with two hands or stops dribbling and starts again. The opposing team gets the ball.

field goal: a successful shot worth 2 points—3 points if shot from behind the three-point line.

foul: called by the officials for breaking a rule: reaching in, blocking, charging, and over the back, for example. If a player commits six fouls during the game, he fouls out and must leave play. If an offensive player is fouled while shooting, he usually gets two foul shots (one shot if the player's basket counted or three if he was fouled beyond the three-point line).

foul shot: a "free throw," an uncontested shot taken from the foul line (15 feet [4.6 m]) from the basket.

goaltending: when a defensive player touches the ball after it has reached its highest point on the way to the basket. The team on offense gets the points they would have received from the basket. Goaltending is also called on any player, on offense or defense, who slaps the backboard or touches the ball directly above the basket.

jump ball: when an official puts the ball into play by tossing it in the air. Two opposing players try to tip it to their own teammate.

man-to-man defense: when each defensive player guards a single offensive player.

officials: those who monitor the action and call fouls. In the NBA there are three for each game.

point guard: the player who handles the ball most on offense. He brings the ball up the court and tries to create scoring opportunities through passing. Good point guards are quick, good passers, and can see the court well.

power forward: a player whose main jobs are to score from close to the basket and win offensive and defensive rebounds. Good power forwards are tall and strong.

rebound: when a player gains possession of the ball after a missed shot.

roster: the players on a team. NBA teams have 12-player rosters.

shooting guard: a player whose main job is to score using jump shots and drives to the basket. Good shooting guards are usually taller than point guards but still quick.

shot clock: a 24-second clock that starts counting down when a team gets the ball. The clock restarts whenever the ball changes possession. If the offense does not shoot the ball in time, it turns the ball over to the other team.

small forward: a player whose main job is to score from inside or outside. Good small forwards are taller than point or shooting guards and have speed and agility.

steal: when a defender takes the ball from an opposing player.

technical foul: called by the official for misconduct or a procedural violation. The team that does not commit the foul gets possession of the ball and a free throw.

three-point play: a two-point field goal combined with a successful free throw. This happens when an offensive player makes a basket but is fouled in the process.

three-point shot: a field goal made from behind the three-point line.

traveling: when a player moves, taking three steps or more, without dribbling, also called "walking." The opposing team gets the ball.

turnover: when the offensive team loses the ball: passing the ball out of bounds, traveling, or double dribbling, for example.

zone defense: when each defensive player guards within a specific area of the court. Common zones include 2-1-2, 1-3-1, or 2-3. Zone defense has only recently been allowed in the NBA.

FURTHER READING

Fishman, John M. *Sports All-Stars: Giannis Antetokounmpo*. Minneapolis: Lerner Publications, 2018.

Goodman, Michael E. *NBA Champions: Milwaukee Bucks*. Mankato, MN : Creative Company, 2018.

Machajewski, Susan. *Giannis Antetokounmpo*. New York: The Rosen Publishing Group, 2018.

Nehm, Eric. *100 Things Bucks Fans Should Know & Do Before They Die*. Chicago: Triumph Books, 2018.

Whiting, Jim. *The NBA: A History of Hoops: Milwaukee Bucks*. Mankato, MN : Creative Company, 2017.

INTERNET RESOURCES

https://www.basketball-reference.com/players/a/antetgi01.html
The basketball-specific resource provided by Sports Reference LLC for current and historical statistics of Giannis Antetokounmpo.

http://bleacherreport.com/nba
The official website for Bleacher Report Sport's NBA reports on each of the 30 teams.

https://www.cbssports.com/nba/teams/MIL/milwaukee-bucks/
The web page for the Milwaukee Bucks provided by CBSSports.com, providing latest news and information, player profiles, scheduling, and standings.

https://www.jsonline.com/sports/bucks/
The web page of *The Milwaukee Journal-Sentinel* newspaper for the Milwaukee Bucks basketball team.

http://www.espn.com/nba/team/_/name/mil/milwaukee-bucks
The official website of ESPN sports network for the Milwaukee Bucks.

http://www.nba.com/#/
The official website of the National Basketball Association.

https://www.nba.com/bucks/
The official NBA website for the Milwaukee Bucks basketball team, including history, player information, statistics, and news.

https://sports.yahoo.com/nba/
The official website of Yahoo! Sports NBA coverage, providing news, statistics, and important information about the association and its 30 teams.

INDEX

INDEX

INDEX

EDUCATIONAL VIDEO LINKS

Pg. 12: http://x-qr.net/1HvM

Pg. 13: http://x-qr.net/1KXW

Pg. 14: http://x-qr.net/1Lbq

Pg. 15: http://x-qr.net/1LvU

Pg. 16: http://x-qr.net/1Ju5

Pg. 17: http://x-qr.net/1J5J

Pg. 18: http://x-qr.net/1KXA

Pg. 19: http://x-qr.net/1JHC

Pg. 32: http://x-qr.net/1JmK

Pg. 47: http://x-qr.net/1LJm

Pg. 58: http://x-qr.net/1JEY

Pg. 70: http://x-qr.net/1M0e

PHOTO CREDITS

Chapter 1:
PA Images / Alamy Stock Photo
Keith Allison / Flickr
Erik Drost / Flickr
Justin Smith / Wikimedia Commons

Chapter 2:
Keith Allison / Flickr
sixtwelve / Flickr
Erik Drost / Flickr
Tuomas Vitikainen / Wikimedia Commons
© Dennis Dolkens | Dreamstime.com
© Martin Ellis | Dreamstime.com
© Debra Saucedo | Dreamstime.com
© Torsak | Dreamstime.com

Chapter 3:
Jose Garcia / Flickr
Keith Allison / Flickr
Richard Bartlaga / Flickr
Keith Allison / Flickr
Mike Clarens/ Wikimedia Commons
Keith Allison / Flickr
182407332_Heat_Sixers0877/Flickr

Chapter 4:
Keith Allison / Flickr
Keith Allison / Flickr
Richard Bartlaga / Flickr
Keith Allison / Flickr
© Martin Ellis | Dreamstime.com
Keith Allison / Flickr

Chapter 5:
Pete Souza / Wikimedia Commons
© Halpland | Dreamstime.com
Gillfoto / Wikimedia Commons
Frank Bryan / Wikimedia Commons
Keith Allison / Flickr
© Shuo Wang | Dreamstime.com

AUTHOR BIOGRAPHY

Donald Parker is an avid sports fan, author, and father. He enjoys watching and participating in many types of sports, including football, basketball, baseball, and golf. He enjoyed a brief career as a punter and defensive back at NCAA Division III Carroll College (now University) in Waukesha, Wisconsin, and spends much of his time now watching and writing about the sports he loves.

NOV   2019